If God Is Always Speaking

Why Can I Not Hear His Voice?

BJ Jenkins

Illustrated by Alicia Estis

Presented to:

_____

By:

_____

Date:

_____

If God Is Always Speaking Why Can I NOT Hear His Voice? **by BJ Jenkins**

Illustrated by Alicia Estis

Copyright © 2020 BJ Jenkins

ISBN 9781953229199

ELIJAH KIDS
PUBLISHING

Elijah Kids Publishing   211 South Madison St. Kosciusko, Mississippi 39090

Special Thanks:

To the Holy Spirit who inspired the idea
and every word of this book and who helped
me to make the deep things of God simple

To Alicia Estis for her dedication in
editing this book so it could be published

There is a God in Heaven who created you and me. Some think He is invisible because He's hard to see.

But anyone can see Him
if they really just believe.
For God is always with us
and will never, ever leave.

And He is always speaking.

He has a lot to say.

There are things He'd like to tell

you each and every day.

But if God is always speaking, why can't you hear His voice? Do you think that you're not old enough to even have a choice?

Is He even listening

when you call out His Name?

Do you think it's something

you did wrong,

and you're the one to blame?

Or does He speak a language that you cannot understand, like people do in places like China and Japan?

If not, there must be

something wrong

we cannot figure out

if you do not HEAR a single word,

a whisper, or a shout!

The truth is, God IS speaking, and He's calling out to YOU. The problem's NOT with Him. The problem is with You!

Most of us are busy folks

with so much on our plate

that we hardly ever take the time

to just sit down and wait.

But waiting is the secret,

the very special thing

that opens up the door

to an audience with the King.

God is King of all the universe,

and He sits upon the throne.

He created all mankind,

so He wouldn't be alone.

Just like He talked with Adam
in the garden long ago,
He wants to talk with everyone
more than you'll ever know.

The King already knows you
and has forgiven you from sin.
HE prepared this place for you
and will gladly let you in.

So right now, why not open up your heart and let Him in? Ask Jesus to come live in you and forgive you from your sin.

Now when you're in His presence,

you must be very still.

Quiet all your inner thoughts

and listen close until...

you hear Him speaking to you.

It won't be blasting loud.

No drums, or horns, or microphones,

or lightning from a cloud.

Although He spoke in thunders

in days of long ago,

today He speaks so softly

most people never know.

Go find somewhere really quiet

to be all alone until

you can train yourself to wait on God

while being very still.

The Holy Spirit speaks to us
deep inside our heart.
Learning how to hear Him there
is the perfect place to start.

Another place you hear His voice

is when you read the Bible,

at Children's Church,

in Sunday School,

and even in Revival.

God even speaks through people,

your parents, or a teacher.

And surely you will hear from God

on Sunday through the preacher.

So everybody lean in close

with your listening ear.

Because God is ALWAYS speaking.

He's speaking loud and clear!

The

End

The NOT Series by BJ Jenkins

The NOT Series, by BJ Jenkins, is a series of books that teach subjects such as the Fruit of the Spirit, Prayer, Hearing the Voice of God, what will be happening in these Last Days, and the story of Jesus.

These books are available as a Rhyming Book, Curriculum, and a Prayer Journal.

Order today at www.bjjenkinsministries.com

Based on the Best Selling Books

These books teach subjects like: What happens when we wait on God, how to hear God's voice, the proper way to pray, the 9 gifts of the Spirit, how to have your spiritual eyes opened, how to be translated in the Spirit, The 7 Horns anointings, and the powers of the age to come.

These books are available as a Rhyming Book, Curriculum, and a Prayer Journal

for E-BOOK ONLY www.jesusministries.com & www.bjjenkinsministries.com

All BOOK Titles offer these options!

Rhyming Book

Rhyming Book—These fun children's rhyming books are illustrated in full color and measure 8 1/2" x 8 1/2". They are easy to read and teach the deep things of God in a simple way even a child can understand. These books are also a great introduction to the curriculum. For Kids Pre-school and Up

Curriculum

Learning Curriculum—These books are printed in full color and measure 8 1/2" x 11". They contain full lesson plans complete with lessons, exercises, games, and even use a puppet to encourage the children. These lessons do not require any advance preparation or study and are designed to be read straight from the pages. For Kids K-12 (and even adults)

Prayer Journal

Prayer Journal—These books are full color and measure 6" x 9". This is a companion to the curriculum. The children are encouraged to journal during each lesson and record what they hear the Lord saying to them. Each lesson has a memory verse, important things to remember, a place to draw pictures, and plenty of room to journal their thoughts. At the end of each chapter, there is a prayer or exercise for the children that will help re-enforce each subject. For Kids K-12

Puppets & Music

Each series also offers a unique puppet that is used along with the curriculum to introduce each lesson. We also offer a CD with music and character voices.

CPSIA information can be obtained
at www.ICGtesting.com
Printed in the USA
BVHW021139030422
633067BV00002B/3